# medieval town

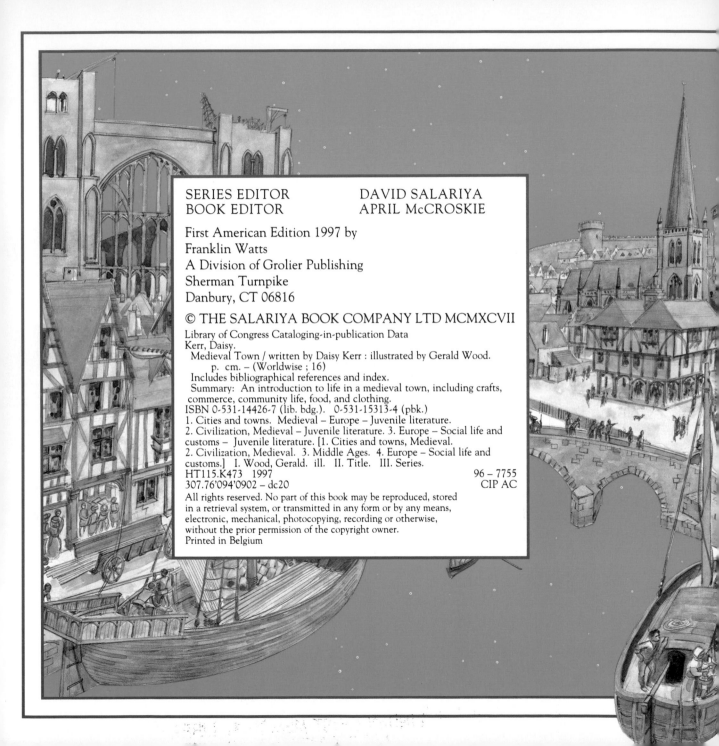

SERIES EDITOR     DAVID SALARIYA
BOOK EDITOR     APRIL McCROSKIE

First American Edition 1997 by
Franklin Watts
A Division of Grolier Publishing
Sherman Turnpike
Danbury, CT 06816

© THE SALARIYA BOOK COMPANY LTD MCMXCVII
Library of Congress Cataloging-in-publication Data
Kerr, Daisy.
  Medieval Town / written by Daisy Kerr : illustrated by Gerald Wood.
    p.  cm. – (Worldwise ; 16)
  Includes bibliographical references and index.
  Summary:  An introduction to life in a medieval town, including crafts,
commerce, community life, food, and clothing.
ISBN 0-531-14426-7 (lib. bdg.).   0-531-15313-4 (pbk.)
1. Cities and towns.  Medieval – Europe – Juvenile literature.
2. Civilization, Medieval – Juvenile literature. 3. Europe – Social life and
customs – Juvenile literature. [1. Cities and towns, Medieval.
2. Civilization, Medieval.  3. Middle Ages.  4. Europe – Social life and
customs.]  I. Wood, Gerald. ill.  II. Title.  III. Series.
HT115.K473  1997                 96 – 7755
307.76'094'0902 – dc20            CIP AC
Printed in Belgium

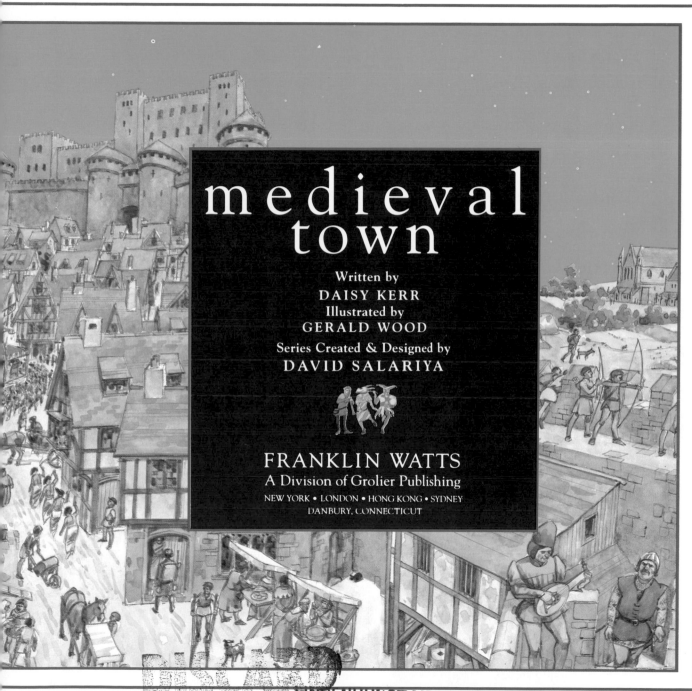

# medieval town

Written by
**DAISY KERR**
Illustrated by
**GERALD WOOD**
Series Created & Designed by
**DAVID SALARIYA**

## FRANKLIN WATTS
A Division of Grolier Publishing
NEW YORK • LONDON • HONG KONG • SYDNEY
DANBURY, CONNECTICUT

# CONTENTS

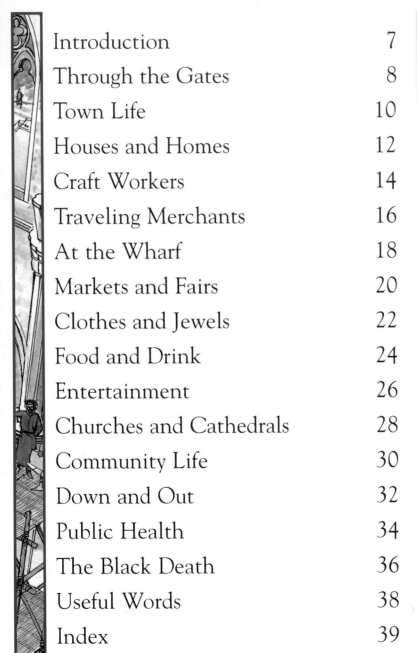

# In the Middle Ages (around A.D. 500-1500),

most people lived and worked in the countryside. Even so, medieval towns were very important, as centers of trade and for defense.

Some of the earliest towns were built like forts. They sheltered the king's soldiers and government officials. Other towns began as markets, where local people traded.

By present-day standards, many medieval towns were small, with less than 1,000 citizens. But a few towns grew into big cities, with 10,000 inhabitants or more.

**Guards marched** along the city walls, keeping a lookout for strangers. The town gates were locked as soon as it became dark. Inside the gates, watchmen patrolled all night. They called out the time every hour.

Towns were favorite targets for enemy attack. They were full of rich prizes to capture – gold and silver crosses from churches, clothes, jewels, and furniture from big houses, silks and spices from warehouses, carvings and tapestries from craft workshops, and hoards of coins from banks.

Towns needed thick walls and strong gates to keep out attackers. Walls and gates also made it difficult for criminals to enter – or to escape with their loot. For extra defense, water-filled moats, earth ramparts (steep banks), and deep ditches were dug all around.

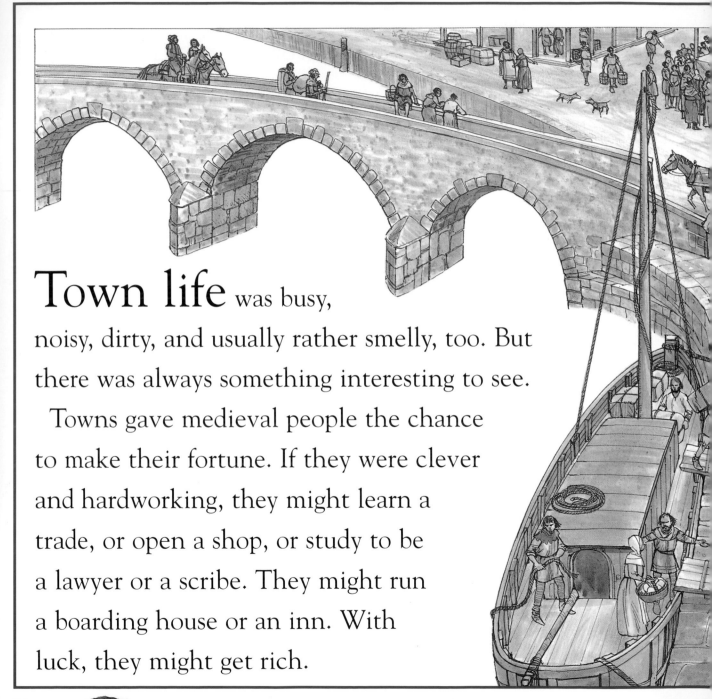

# Town life was busy,

noisy, dirty, and usually rather smelly, too. But there was always something interesting to see.

Towns gave medieval people the chance to make their fortune. If they were clever and hardworking, they might learn a trade, or open a shop, or study to be a lawyer or a scribe. They might run a boarding house or an inn. With luck, they might get rich.

**Countrywomen** walked long distances into town. They set up stalls in streets, selling goods like eggs, fruit, and herbs from their gardens and farms.

# Early townhouses

were small and simple. As towns became richer, houses got larger, with carved timbers, stained glass, and decorated plasterwork. Roofs were covered in fireproof clay tiles.

There was often not much empty space within town walls. So houses were built several stories high, with shops underneath. Poor families lived together in just one room.

Sleeping area

Embroiderer

Weaver

Tailor

**Shops** were opened in citizens' front rooms. Goods were sold from a counter at the window.

Farmers drove sheep into the town to sell them at the market. Town councils made laws about controlling the animals, but they were often ignored.

Stone carver

Glazier

Carpenter

Tapestry maker

Weaver

Coin maker

Goldsmith

*Apprentices help an alchemist (scientist) with his experiments.*

**Boys** (and a few girls) learned craft skills by becoming apprentices. When they were about 8 years old, they went to live with a master craftsman and his family. The master provided food, clothes, and lodging, and he taught them his craft skills.

**After 7 years,** apprentices qualified as fully trained "journeymen." If they were very skilled, they could qualify as a master by making a fine example of their work, called a "masterpiece." If other masters thought the work was good, the journeyman was accepted as a new master.

Sheep shearer

Dyer

Fuller

Lantern maker

Thimble maker

Harness maker

Metal worker

Artist

Ivory carver

Embroiderer

Glass blower

Potter

Cobbler

Blacksmith

# In the Middle Ages, almost everything was made by hand. There were only a few simple machines, like potter's wheels and weaving looms, to help. So everyone relied on craft workers' skills. Craft goods ranged from delicate gold jewelry and fragile glass, to heavy iron cauldrons and thick leather boots.

Most craft workers lived in towns. Each craft had its own guild. Craft guilds inspected work, asked for better wages, and helped members who were ill.

Pewter worker

Nail maker

Candle maker

Knife grinder

Tailor

Armorer

Locksmith

*These well-armed 14th-century merchants are carrying gold (on camels) across the Sahara Desert from the rich African kingdom of Mali.*

**Muslim merchants** traveled through Asia, North Africa, and the Middle East. They sold porcelain from China and pottery from Turkey and Iran (*right*).

**The merchant** city of Venice, Italy, was a great center of international trade.

**The rarest,** most valuable goods were sold from showrooms in merchants' homes. Other imported goods were sold from stalls in the town streets.

*In Venice you could buy silk from China, precious stones from India, and perfumes from Arabia.*

Ginger

Nutmeg

Mace

Peppercorns

Cardamom

Vanilla pods

**Spices** came from India and the islands of Southeast Asia. They were highly prized in medieval times.

Silk Route

Black Sea

Central Asia

China

Africa   Arabia   India

# Some medieval

merchants spent their whole lives traveling. They braved steep mountain paths, howling deserts, and stormy oceans – as well as hunger, sunstroke, and disease – to bring valuable goods to European towns from Africa, India, and the Far East. Why did they risk their lives? They needed to bring goods to towns, but some loved adventure; some were curious to see new sights and meet new people in distant lands. Others hoped to grow rich.

**The Silk Route** was a network of tracks running overland through wild, dangerous country. It stretched from China through central Asia to the Black Sea. Merchants from many lands traveled along it, buying goods to take back to town.

# The largest and most successful towns were

*Ships unloaded their cargo at the town wharf. Town officials collected taxes and customs duties on incoming goods.*

built close to water. In the Middle Ages, water was the best way of carrying heavy, bulky loads. There were no trucks, trains, or planes, and travel by road was slow.

During the Middle Ages, many different ships were designed for various transporting purposes. Warships were built with platforms, for fighting, at each end. Merchant ships had deep, wide hulls for carrying lots of cargo.

**Travel by sea** could be dangerous. Shipwrecks were common and pirates lurked in coastal waters, waiting to raid merchant ships.

**Ships** for gusty northern seas were powered by wind trapped in big square sails. Ships for the calm Mediterranean Sea were mostly rowed with oars.

*13th-century warship*

*13th-century "round" ship*

*14th-century merchant cog*

*13th-century war galley*

*15th-century Flemish carrack*

Bread

Eggs

Cloth

Most towns held a market at least once a week. In big towns, every day (except Sunday) was market day. And there might be separate marketplaces – fish market, cattle market, hay market – for different kinds of goods. Fairs were held at festival times, such as Easter and Midsummer.

**Market officials** inspected goods on sale to check their quality and value.

Big fairs attracted merchants and customers from all over Europe. There were hundreds of stalls, sideshows, and fields with tents where visitors could stay. Traveling storytellers, acrobats, minstrels, and jugglers entertained the crowds.

*Fish*

Elaborate
hairstyle

Hood

Merchants, bankers,
and other wealthy
citizens wore clothes
like this in the late
14th century.

**The merchant**
proudly carries
a purse full of
money slung from
his belt. His wife
keeps her money
hidden safely
under the folds
of her robe.

Long-sleeved
smock worn
under woman's
robe

Getting dressed
was simple
around
1450: first a
loose smock
(tunic) and
breeches (pants)
of linen. Then
hose (like leggings)
made of wool
cloth – a separate
one for each leg.
A codpiece
(cloth flap)
covered the gap
at the top,
between the hose.
Finally, a jerkin
(sleeveless jacket)
and, if cold,
a cloak.

Purse

Long-toed shoes

Spurs

Priests, monks, and
nuns wore simple
wool robes.

1350            1450

*Peasants and ordinary townfolk wore plain, simple clothes, made of longwearing home-spun wool or linen cloth. They were loose, for comfort while working.*

**Medieval clothes** were expensive. A long robe or cloak used many yards of cloth. Also, all clothes were made slowly and carefully by hand – from spinning and weaving the thread to sewing the seams.

**Clothes worn** by wealthy people could be very elaborate. Like today, fashions changed from time to time. Above, you can see a selection of clothes, hats, shoes, and jewelry worn by rich citizens from approximately 1350 to around 1450.

# Townspeople liked fine clothes.

Rich merchants and their wives wore long fur-lined velvet robes, embroidered with colored silk and real gold thread.

Craftsmen wore longwearing tunics and cloth hose dyed in bright colors. Their wives wore linen scarves and belts trimmed with gold and jewels. Children in wealthy families wore miniature versions of adult clothes. Poor citizens had homemade garments, secondhand clothes, or castoffs.

# Townsfolk had a wider choice of food than countryfolk. Fruit, vegetables, meat, poultry, and fish could be bought at the market. Sugar, dates, raisins, and spices were imported from distant lands. There were bakers' shops, cake stalls, alehouses and wine cellars. In big townhouses, meat was roasted over open fires and puddings were baked in brick-lined ovens.

**A wealthy person's** kitchen might have foods like eggs, herbs, rabbit, sacks of flour, and jugs of wine.

*Bakers caught selling moldy loaves were dragged through the streets as a punishment.*

Hot takeout food – like meat pies – were baked in portable ovens. Few people had an oven at home.

**Ordinary citizens'** food was simple but filling, like pea pottage:
1. Soak some dried peas in water overnight.
2. Put them in a big pot with lots of water, some herbs, garlic, onions, cabbage, a ham bone, or some bacon rinds.
3. Cook slowly until you have a thick soup.
4. Eat with bread and cheese.

There were no refrigerators or freezers to store fresh food. Fish was preserved by drying, salting, or pickling in vinegar.

Meals were a way of entertaining important business contacts. Families ate together, too. Children had to have good table manners.

Hunters and trappers from the countryside trudged into the town to sell the birds, rabbits and hares they had caught.

KITCHEN
EQUIPMENT
1. Cooking pots
2. Water jug
3. Knives
4. Jugs for ale

1.

2.

3.

4.

Mummers put on animal masks and danced wildly through the streets, playing music, at Christmastime.

Members of craft guilds staged mystery plays, which retold famous stories from the Bible.

**Mummers** sang songs based on ancient legends. Citizens gave them food or money – if not, the mummers attacked them.

Nativity play

**At great religious festivals,** especially Easter, plays were staged inside churches and cathedrals. Monks acted out important events in the life of Jesus Christ. The choir sang specially composed chants and hymns.

**The first nativity** plays, telling the story of Jesus' birth, were performed in the Middle Ages.

*Mummers played many different musical instruments. Left to right: viol, nackers, shawm, drum, bagpipes, hurdy-gurdy, lute, double flute.*

Medieval townspeople had many ways to have fun. There were holidays on saints' days, carnival processions with music and dancing, plays and puppet shows, and entertainers in the streets.

For peaceful relaxation, there were public bathhouses or private gardens. After work, men and women gathered in taverns (bars) to chat, drink ale, eat bread and roasted apples, and play dice or cards.

**Soccer** was a very popular sport – and often very violent, too. It was played in the streets, with a pig's bladder for a ball.

*Pig's bladder*

*Bear baiting was a sport we condemn as very cruel today. Fierce dogs attacked a chained and muzzled bear.*

# Religious ceremonies

played an important part in town life. People went to church services at least once a week, as well as on special occasions, like weddings and funerals.

People gave money to the Church for fine new buildings and for charity work. Priests and monks ran schools and colleges, and nuns offered wise advice.

*Pilgrims made long journeys to visit shrines (holy places) in medieval towns. They bought badges, like this shell, as souvenirs.*

**A cathedral** was a special type of church, ruled by a bishop. It was the bishop's job to make sure all the churches in his area were run properly and that all priests, monks, and nuns behaved well.

**Splendid** cathedrals were built in many big cities, to glorify God and increase the city's importance.

# It was not an easy task to govern a medieval town. There were many tensions between rich and poor, local people and visitors, and between workers and the unemployed. Gangs rioted in the streets, and there were robbers and muggers.

There were quarrels in the marketplace. Traders accused one another of lying, cheating, or refusing to pay their debts.

*Heretics were people accused of crimes against the Church. They were burned alive at a wooden stake.*

*Petty criminals were put in the stocks for a couple of hours. People jeered at them and threw sticks and stones.*

*Some councils drove criminals and beggars out of town.*

**Town council** members (*right*) were leading merchants, bankers, lawyers, and landlords.

# In most medieval towns,
you would meet very few rich people and a great many poor. There were down-and-outs everywhere: mothers and children begged in the gutter, and exhausted men huddled in doorways or stayed among the straw in stables and backyards.

Most of these people were homeless and poor because they could not find work, or were weak, old, or ill. There were no state benefits in medieval times. If people's families and friends could not help them, they might starve. So they tramped into town from the countryside, hoping that rich people would give them money or food.

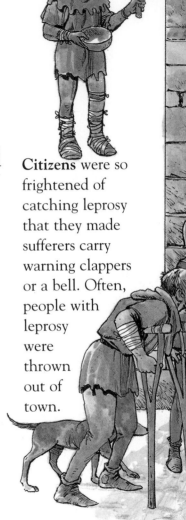

**Citizens** were so frightened of catching leprosy that they made sufferers carry warning clappers or a bell. Often, people with leprosy were thrown out of town.

**Leprosy** was a serious skin disease that led to disability and death.

**The Church** taught that rich people should share their wealth. Life was uncertain and maybe one day they would be poor. Then it would be their turn to beg.

**Rich citizens** sent their servants with baskets of leftovers to feed poor people at the town gates.

*Big cities had regular handouts of bread to poor people during food shortages.*

**This chart** (*right*), from a medieval medical textbook, was designed to help doctors study patients' urine to try to find out the cause of their illness.

*Doctors said that too much blood was bad for you. They used leeches (water slugs) to suck out the extra blood.*

*Few townhouses had toilets like this. People used a bucket, or a pit full of earth. Officials told citizens to dump waste outside the town walls.*

Almost half the babies born in medieval towns died before they were five years old. A few died from accidents, but mostly they died from illnesses. Town streets and waterways were full of rotting garbage – great breeding places for germs and disease. Deadly diseases also passed easily from one person to another in crowded houses and shops.

Town councils tried to make citizens keep their environment clean and healthy, but without much success.

*The nuns' hospital at Beaune, France*

**Trepanning** was supposed to cure madness, epilepsy, or severe headaches. But most patients died.

*Trepanning (cutting a hole in the skull) was a very dangerous operation.*

**Nuns** ran many hospitals. Patients were given good food, medicine, and nursing care. Treatment was free to the poor.

*The Church forbade cutting up dead bodies but doctors still studied anatomy. These medieval drawings show a baby inside its mother.*

*Dentist*

**Dentists** pulled out rotten teeth using huge iron pincers. Alcohol and mixtures of herbs were used as painkillers.

*Midwife*

**In childbirth,** most townswomen were cared for by midwives. Ordinary people could not afford doctors' fees.

*Bleeding (making a cut in a vein to let the blood run out) was a popular treatment for many common illnesses. It did not do any good.*

# The Black Death was a

deadly illness. It killed almost half the families in Europe between 1347 and 1351. Symptoms included painful swellings under the arms, a burning fever, and a purple rash. Outbreaks were particularly bad in towns. Sadly, there was nothing medieval doctors could do. The dead were buried quickly in deep pits. Often priests and gravediggers caught the disease and died.

*The Black Death was spread by rat fleas. The fleas bit humans and introduced deadly germs into the blood.*

**Flagellants** (people with whips) thought the Black Death was caused by their sins. They hit themselves and asked God to forgive them.

*Flea*

# USEFUL WORDS

**Alchemist** A medieval scientist who also studied magic. Alchemists tried to find the formula for turning ordinary metal into gold.

**Black Death** A deadly disease, spread by rat fleas.

**Codpiece** Flap of cloth joining the two legs of a pair of hose together at the top.

**Epilepsy** A disorder of the nervous system.

**Fuller** Worker who processed newly woven wool.

**Guild** Association of craftworkers, all doing the same kind of work.

**Journeyman** Fully trained craft-worker.

**Leeches** Blood-sucking water slugs.

**Leprosy** A serious skin disease, which slowly eats away fingers and toes. Today it is curable by drugs.

**Mummers** Ordinary people who put on animal masks and sang and danced.

**Mystery plays** Plays on a religious theme, performed by members of craft guilds.

**Pewter** A silvery metal, used for dishes and mugs.

**Pottage** Thick soup.

**Sheep shearer** Worker who cut (sheared) the wool from sheep.

**Stocks** A wooden trap that held people by the head and arms. Used in public as a punishment.

**Tapestry** Pictures woven from wool.

**Trepanning** Making holes in the skull to try to cure illnesses.

# INDEX